Gal GADOT

Joanne Mattern

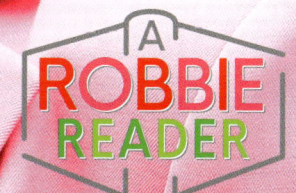

A ROBBIE READER

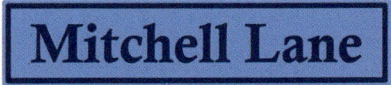

PUBLISHERS

2001 SW 31st Avenue
Hallandale, FL 33009

www.mitchelllane.com

Copyright © 2020 by Mitchell Lane Publishers. All rights reserved. No part of this book may be reproduced without written permission from the publisher. Printed and bound in the United States of America.

First Edition, 2020.
Author: Joanne Mattern
Designer: Ed Morgan
Editor: Lisa Petrillo

Series: Robbie Reader
Title: Gal Godot / by Joanne Mattern

Hallandale, FL : Mitchell Lane Publishers, [2020]

Library bound ISBN: 9781680205121
eBook ISBN: 9781680205138

PHOTO CREDITS: Design Elements, freepik.com, APImages.com

Contents

one
A **RELUCTANT WINNER** — 4

two
An **ACTIVE CHILDHOOD** — 8

three
From **SOLDIER** to **ACTRESS** — 12

four
A **FAST** and **FURIOUS** Ride — 16

five
A **REAL-LIFE WONDER WOMAN** — 22

Timeline	28
Find Out More	29
Works Consulted	29
About the Author	32

CHAPTER ONE

A Reluctant Winner

Gal Gadot was not happy. She had entered the 2004 Miss Israel **beauty pageant** because it had seemed like a fun thing to do. "I thought it'd be cool to tell my grandkids that grandma was in the Miss Israel pageant," she told a reporter from *Glamour* fashion magazine.

During the pageant, Gadot was interviewed by judges. She had to give her opinion about many subjects. She walked down a fashion show runway modeling evening gowns. She even had to sing and perform onstage. All the while, judges watched everything she did.

To her surprise, Gadot won the pageant. Gadot was excited, but she was also very scared. Being Miss Israel was a big job. She had to represent her country around the world. She visited schools. She made speeches. She raised money for charity. Gadot didn't really mind doing these things. The problem was that winning Miss Israel meant she would compete in the Miss Universe pageant. And Gadot definitely did not want to win that contest!

Miss Israel Gal Gadot in 2004

CHAPTER ONE

Gadot decided she would do everything she could to lose the pageant. She showed up late to events. She did not wear makeup or fix her hair. She refused to wear gowns to some events. "I was very naughty. I'm a really good girl but because I was afraid I would win again. I came late in all the rehearsals and I wasn't wearing the right evening gowns."

To her relief, Gadot did not win the Miss Universe title. Now she was free to get on with her life. Gadot had many big plans. She would join the military. She would go to college and get a job as a lawyer. However, Gadot's life did not turn out the way she expected. The next few years would be full of surprises.

A Reluctant Winner

Gadot as Miss Israel waves at photographers as she competed for the Miss Universe contest in 2004.

CHAPTER TWO

An *Active* Childhood

Gal Godot (gah-DOHT) was born on April 30, 1985, in Rosh Ha'Ayin, Israel. Her father, Michael, is an **engineer**. Her mother, Init, is a physical education teacher. Gal is the older child, with a younger sister named Dana.

Gadot in 2009

From her earliest days, young Gal loved to be the center of attention. She told a reporter from *Vanity Fair* magazine, "My mom told me that when I was three, they threw a party on the rooftop of the house. They put me to bed, and I heard people coming into the house and no one came to me. I went to the rooftop and took a hose and I started to spray water on everyone, just to get attention." She called out to the guests, "Look at meee!"

CHAPTER **TWO**

The Gadots were an active family. Gal and Dana spent most of their free time outside. Gadot told ESPN, "My mom is amazing. Because of her, I was so active my entire life. There was no TV time. There was, 'Take the ball and go outside and play.'"

Growing up, Gal especially loved to dance. She studied different kinds of dance for twelve years, including jazz, ballet, hip-hop, and modern dance. She also competed in sports such as basketball, tennis, swimming, and volleyball.

Along with sports, the Gadot family enjoyed entertainment. "In the evening after having dinner, we used to sit down and watch movies," Gadot told a reporter from the British magazine *Bring the Noise*. "On the weekends, they used to take my sister and me to the theater." These trips gave Gadot a love of movies and drama. "I always had the passion but I was not aware of it," she admitted.

An Active Childhood

Gadot worked several jobs when she became a teenager. She babysat for neighbors. Later she worked at Burger King. A few times, **talent scouts** asked her to do some modeling, but Gadot was not interested. Gadot still loved to dance and dreamed of being a **choreographer**. But first, she had to serve her country.

Gadot attends the Gucci Bamboo Fragrance promotional event in July 2015.

CHAPTER THREE

From Soldier to Actress

Every citizen in Israel has to serve in the **military**, and Gadot was no exception. After she graduated from high school, she served two years in the Israel Defense Forces. Since its beginnings in 1948, Israel has faced many wars and military attacks, and its citizens believe in being prepared. "Part of being Israeli is to go to the army," Gadot told a reporter from *People* magazine. "All my friends went, my parents went, and my grandparents went."

Gadot described her time in the army as difficult but rewarding. First she did a four-month boot camp in Israel's hot Negev desert. During this time, Gadot went on seven-mile runs every morning and took part in difficult physical workouts. She also learned how to use different weapons. Later, Gadot became an instructor and trained other soldiers in gymnastics and physical fitness. "Serving in the military is not easy," Gadot told a reporter from the entertainment news website, *NME*. "You give two or three years, and it's not about you. You give your freedom away. You learn discipline and respect."

Gadot was still in the army when a terrorist group from Lebanon called Hezbollah crossed the border and attacked Israel. The Israel-Hezbollah War only lasted a month. During that time, as a soldier, Gadot supported combat troops who fought on the front lines.

Gadot attends the Women of the Israeli Defense Forces Celebration in June 2007.

CHAPTER THREE

When Gadot's military service ended, she enrolled in Reichman Law School. She also did some modeling. Gadot wasn't in school for long because a movie director saw a photograph of her from her modeling agency. The director asked Gadot to try out for a part as a Bond girl in the new James Bond film, *Quantum of Solace*.

At first, Gadot said no. "I said, 'I'm studying law and international relations. I'm way too serious and smart to be an actress.'" Gadot also worried that the script was in English, which she did not speak very well. Gadot soon changed her mind and **auditioned**, but she did not get the part. Still, the experience helped her realize she really liked the idea of acting.

Gadot dropped out of college and studied acting. In 2007, she was cast in an Israeli TV series called *Bubot*, a drama about the modeling world. Even bigger roles were about to come her way.

CHAPTER **FOUR**

A Fast and Furious Ride

Gadot had just started acting in *Bubot* when another offer came her way. She was asked to audition for a role in the fourth *Fast & Furious* movie. This series of big-budget Hollywood movies had begun in 2001 and focused on the exciting and dangerous world of illegal street racing. Gadot was cast as Gisele Yashar in the *Fast & Furious* movie in 2009.

Gadot handles her growing fame going from law student to fashion model to movie star.

Gadot loved appearing in the movie. Her military training and physical fitness were a great help in filming the movie's many action-filled scenes. Gadot insisted on doing most of her own stunts. "I enjoyed being able to do the stuff that in real life you can't," Gadot told a reporter for *Real Style Network*. "I want to fly up in the air, on the motorcycle, whatever. I want to do it all myself."

CHAPTER **FOUR**

She also enjoyed working with the film's stars, including Vin Diesel, Paul Walker, and Michelle Rodriguez. "We all have such a great chemistry, it really shows on screen," she told the Website From the Grapevine.com.

Gadot appears at premiere of her film in the *Fast & Furious* franchise.

A Fast and Furious Ride

Gal Gadot and Yaron Versano arrive at the 75th Golden Globe Awards in January 2018.

Gadot's personal life was also exciting. In 2008, she married a Dutch businessman named Yaron Versano. In 2011, the couple welcomed their daughter Alma.

CHAPTER **FOUR**

Chris *Ludacris* Bridges, Gadot, and Vin Diesel pose at the after party for the premiere of *Fast & Furious 6* in May 2013.

Gadot appeared in three more *Fast & Furious* movies before her character was killed in 2015's *Furious 7*. She also appeared in several other movies and a television miniseries. Then one day, her **agent** called and told her to fly to Los Angeles for a secret role. Gadot did, but even when she auditioned for director Zack Snyder, she had no idea what the part was. Then Snyder asked her if Wonder Woman was popular in Israel. Gadot said the comic book hero definitely was.

A Fast and Furious Ride

Gadot didn't hear any news about the movie for six weeks. Finally, she got a call telling her that she had won the role of Wonder Woman in the movie *Batman v. Superman: Dawn of Justice*. The 2016 movie starred well-known actors Ben Affleck and Henry Cavill, and introduced Wonder Woman as a character. Gadot was thrilled to be playing such as strong, independent woman.

Batman v. Superman did not do well with fans or **critics**. However, people loved Gadot's performance. They couldn't wait to see Wonder Woman in her own film.

Zack Snyder (*left*), Henry Cavill, Ben Affleck, and Gadot pose for photographers promoting *Batman v. Superman: Dawn of Justice* in March 2016.

21

CHAPTER FIVE

A Real-Life Wonder Woman

Gadot was in good physical shape, but playing Wonder Woman meant she had to be even tougher. Before she started filming, Gadot went through six months of training. Her workouts included martial arts, sword fighting, kickboxing, and horseback riding. Gadot said the training was even tougher than her days in the Israeli military!

To make things even harder, Gadot was expecting her second child. After most of the movie was finished, she had to reshoot a few scenes. To hide her changing body, she covered her stomach with a green cloth. Later, her body was digitally changed so it matched her look in the rest of the film. Gadot welcomed her daughter Maya early in 2017.

Wonder Woman became a huge hit and Gadot and her costar, Chris Pine, were the center of attention. The film earned more than $700 million around the world, more than many other superhero movies.

Chris Pine with Gadot

CHAPTER **FIVE**

Gadot was especially happy about playing such a strong, positive character. In January 2018, Gadot won a Critics' Choice Award, an annual award voted on by journalists. She told the audience, "Throughout my career, I was always asked to describe my dream role. And it was clear to me that I wanted to portray a strong and independent woman—a real one. Later, I was cast as Wonder Woman, and all of these qualities I looked for, I found in her. She's full of heart, strength, compassion, and forgiveness. She sees wrong that must be made right; she takes action when everyone around her is idle. She commands the attention of the world. And in doing so, she sets a positive example for humanity."

Gadot is the star at premiere of *Wonder Woman*.

CHAPTER FIVE

Despite her fame, Gadot tries to live a normal life with her husband and their children. Her Jewish faith is very important to her. Her family takes part in many Jewish rituals, including lighting the Sabbath candles every Friday night and going to services at the **synagogue**.

Gadot also gives back through charity work. One of her favorite causes is education. She is active with the charity Pencils of Promise, which works to provide equal education for all children around the world. Through her work with Pencils of Promise, Gadot has raised thousands of dollars to build new schools.

Through her acting, Gal Gadot has become a role model for girls and boys. It's a role this real-life Wonder Woman is happy to play, both on and off the screen.

2018 MTV Video Music Awards

Timeline

1985 — Gal Gadot is born on April 30 in Rosh Ha'Ayin, Israel

2004 — Wins Miss Israel pageant, represents Israel in Miss Universe

2005 — Begins required two-year service in the Israeli Defense Forces

2007 — Drops out of college to become an actress; appears on the Israeli TV series *Bubot*

2008 — Gadot marries businessman Yaron Versano

2009 — Gadot plays Gisele Yahar in *Fast & Furious*

2011 — Appears in *Fast Five*; daughter Alma Versano is born

2013 — Appears in *Fast & Furious 6*

2015 — Appears in *Furious 7*

2016 — Gadot plays Wonder Woman in *Batman v. Superman*

2017 — Stars in *Wonder Woman*; gives birth to her second daughter, Maya

2018 — Appears in *Justice League: Part Two*

Find Out More

Orr, Tamra B. *Gal Gadot*. Kennett Square, Pennsylvania: Purple Toad Publishing, 2018.

Sherman, Jill. *Gal Gadot: Soldier, Model, Wonder Woman*. Minneapolis: Lerner Publishing Group, 2018.

Ducksters: "Wonder Woman"
https://www.ducksters.com/biography/wonder_woman.php

Gal Gadot
http://www.galgadot.com

IMDb: "Gal Gadot"
https://www.imdb.com/name/nm2933757/bio?ref_=nm_ov_bio_sm

Superhero Universe: "Wonder Woman"
http://superherouniverse.com/superheroes/wonderwoman.htm

Works Consulted

Bailey, Alyssa. "Read Gal Gadot's Powerful Critics' Choice Award Speech About Equality and 'Wonder Woman." Elle.com, January 11, 2018. https://www.elle.com/culture/celebrities/a15066851/gal-gadot-critics-choice-seeher-award-speech/

Bayley, Leanne. "Gal Gadot: The Woman We'll ALL Be Talking About in June." *Glamour*, May 30, 2017. http://www.glamourmagazine.co.uk/galley/gal-gadot-interview-face-of-gucci-bamboo-fragrance

Beaumont, Mark. "Get to Know Gal Gadot: The Wonder Woman 2017 Needs." NME.com, June 2, 2017. http://www.nme.com/features/gal-gadot-interview-woman-woman-2017-2082497#G15blkk8b5715suE.99

D'Estries, Michael. "Gal Gadot's Rise from Law Student to Supermodel to Movie Star." From the Grapevine.com, June 9, 2017. https://www.fromthegrapevine.com/slideshows/arts/gal-gadot-movies-wonder-woman-batman-vs-superman-israeli-actress-model/page/3

"*Fast & Furious 6* Star Gal Gadot Beauty Interview." Real Style Network.com, May 2013. http://www.realstylenetwork.com/beauty/2013/05/fast-furious-6-star-gal-gadot-beauty-interview

Works Consulted *continued*

"Film Interview: Gal Gadot." BringtheNoiseUK.com, September 2013. http://www.bringthenoiseuk.com/201309/music/interviews/film-interview-gal-gadot-gisele-fast-furious-6

Frigillana, Mikaela. "Gal Gadot Takes a Stance on Education." BorgenMagazine.com, July 28, 2017. https://www.borgenmagazine.com/gal-gadot-takes-a-stance-on-education/

"Gal Gadot Is Wonder Woman" 'She Is Not Relying on a Man, and She's Not There Because of a Love Story.'" *Glamour*, March 7, 2016. https://www.glamour.com/story/gal-gadot-wonder-woman-cover-interview

Glock, Allison. "The Conversation: Actor, Mother, and Superhero Gal Gadot." ESPN.com, May 30, 2017. http://www.espn.com/espnw/culture/article/19496814/actor-mother-superhero-gal-gadot

Heller, Corinne. "Gal Gadot's Pageant Past: Wonder Woman Star Dazzled as Miss Israel." EOnline.com, May 31, 2017. https://www.eonline.com/news/858131/gal-gadot-s-pageant-past-wonder-woman-star-dazzled-as-miss-israel#photo-818805

Jacobs, Laura. "Meet Gal Gadot, Our New Wonder Woman." *Vanity Fair*, August 2015. http://www.vanityfair.com/hollywood/2015/07/gal-gadot-wonder-woman-miss-israel

McNiece, Mia. "How Serving in the Israeli Army Helped Prepare Batman v. Superman's Gal Gadot to Play Wonder Woman." *People*, March 31, 2016. http://people.com/movies/how-serving-in-the-israeli-army-helped-prepare-gal-gadot-for-wonder-woman/

Sperling, Nicole. "Gal Gadot Did Reshoots for Wonder Woman While Pregnant." *Entertainment Weekly*, April 25, 2017. http://ew.com/movies/2017/04/25/gal-gadot-wonder-woman-reshoots-pregnant/

Glossary

agent
A person who represents someone in business

auditioned
Tried out for a part in a movie or play

beauty pageant
A show in which people dress up and perform to win a prize

choreographer
A person who designs a dance

critics
People who judge a TV show or other entertainment

engineer
A person who designs or builds something using scientific principles

military
Armed forces that defend a country

synagogue
A building for Jewish worship

talent scouts
People whose job is to find talented performers for shows or movies

Index

Batman v. Superman: Dawn of Justice	21
Bubot	14, 16
Critics' Choice Award	24
Fast & Furious movies	16-18
Gadot, Dana	8
Gadot, Gal	
in beauty pageants	4-6
family of	8
childhood of	9-10
military service of	12-13
attends law school	14
works as a model	14
marries Yaron Versano	19
gives birth to Alma	19
auditions to play *Wonder Woman*	20
appears in *Batman v. Superman*	21
stars in *Wonder Woman*	22-23
gives birth to Maya	23
wins Critics' Choice Award	24
religious faith of	26
charity work of	26
Gadot, Irit	8
Gadot, Michael	8
Israel Defense Forces	12
Israel-Hezbollah War	13
Pencils of Promise	26
Quantum of Solace	14
Snyder, Zach	21
Versano, Yaron	19
Wonder Woman	22-23

About the Author

Joanne Mattern is the author of many books for youths on a variety of subjects. She loves writing biographies for Mitchell Lane publishers about what makes famous people so special. She was thrilled to write about Gal Gadot and show people what a confident and exciting woman this actress is. Mattern lives in New York State with her husband, children, and several pets.